Cold Spring Rising

COLD SPRING RISING

Poems by

John Thomas York

Press 53
Winston-Salem

Press 53, LLC
PO Box 30314
Winston-Salem, NC 27130

First Edition

Copyright © 2012 by John Thomas York

All rights reserved, including the right of reproduction in whole or in part in any form. For permission, contact publisher at editor@Press53.com, or at the address above.

Cover design by Kevin Morgan Watson

Cover art, "Variation of Leaf on Water,"
Copyright © 2012 by Jan Jílek,
used by permission of the artist.

Author photo by Rachel York

Printed on acid-free paper

ISBN 978-1-935708-52-0

*For my daughters,
Elizabeth, Kathryn, and Rachel*

POEM   A cold spring. Sweet water nobody knows is
           there but you. You stand, looking down, and
           see yourself outlined against the sky.

—Jim Wayne Miller, "From the Brier Glossary of Literary Terms"

Acknowledgments

Some of the poems in this book previously appeared in the following: *Appalachian Journal, The Arts Journal, border crossing, Coraddi, Greensboro News and Record, Greensboro Review, Hemlocks and Balsams, International Poetry Review, Kentucky Poetry Review, The Lyricist, Pembroke Magazine, Pinesong, My Laureate's Lasso, South Carolina Review,* and *The Student* (Wake Forest University).

In addition, "Wish" was published in *Tar River Poetry*. "Naming the Constellations" won the Poet Laureate Award from the North Carolina Poetry Society in 2008. "The Loon" won first place in the adult division of Muse on Greensboro, a contest sponsored by the Friends of the Greensboro Public Library, in 2008. "Passing Bear Creek" won first prize in a poetry contest sponsored by *Coraddi* in 1985, while "Johnny's Cosmology" won the Literary Award for Poetry in 1985 from *Greensboro Review*.

"Johnny Flora's Dream of Flying" appeared in the anthology *A gathering at the Forks: Fifteen years of the Hindman Settlement School Appalachian Writers Workshop*. "Eleventh Grade: 1971" appeared in the anthology *Word and Witness: 100 Years of North Carolina Poetry*. "Brains," "June," "Puzzle," and "Egret" appeared in *The Southern Poetry Anthology, Volume III: Contemporary Appalachia*.

The personae in the fourth section, *Donahaw County*, are fictional characters. Any resemblance to any person, living or dead, is accidental.

Contents

Naming the Constellations   1

I. Tall Grass

Irving Street	7
I Dream of Driving a 1949 Two-Ton Chevy Flatbed	9
Wild Turkeys	10
Whippoorwill	11
Brains	12
Bathroom Music	14
O Christmas Tree	15
The Gift	16
June	17
Substitute	18
Sharecroppers	20
Puzzle	22

II. Nebo

The Ghost of Nebo	27
The Captain Disguised as a Twelve-Year-Old Boy	29
Johnny's Cosmology	30
Mowing for Grandmothers:	
1. Grandma Spencer's Yard, Rockford Road	32
2. Granny York, Irving Street	33
Picking Out	34
Eleventh Grade: 1971	35
Nebo	36

III. Always in the Middle of Things

The Death of Superman	39
Meteorites	40

Always in the Middle of Things	41
Cataloochee	42
The Squirrel Woman	43
Lost and Found	45
Shining Wind, Stone, and Tree	46
The Loon	47
Water Lilies, for Jane	50

IV. Donahaw County

Katy's Sunfish	55
Bobby Jester's Dandelion Blues	57
Diana Flora Throwing	59
Johnny Flora's Dream of Flying	61
Tommy "Match" Dalton Takes His Break	62
Joe Stewart's Reservoir	64
Glory Brown, Her Visitors	66
Millie Greenwood, Deciding How to Pray	68
Velmer Dobson's Night Out	70

V. There's a Landscape That Lives

Chasing Diana Most of the Night,	
Driving from Wilmington to Banner Elk, NC	75
Passing Bear Creek	76
A Stout One	77
Barn Swallows	78
Egret	80
Highway 67 and the Old Winston Road	82
Teaching Time	83
A Winter Triptych	
1. Fall Creek, 1960	84
2. Boone, 1973	85
3. Westover Terrace, 2006	87
Wish	89
The Calling	90

Naming the Constellations

1

Trace a line from the front
of the Big Dipper's cup, over to Polaris,
the penny nail on which the Little Dipper swings.
The rest of the sky, even the visible
galaxies fleeing the big bang,
seem to turn on that near nothing of a star.

Then look for Bootes rising
among catalpa blossoms, Aquila hovering
above summer haze, Orion climbing
through bare trees, or the Gemini
watching over hoar-frosted mountaintops.
Even if we never wander over desert places

nor through winter woods at night,
we need to learn the old names,
Ursa Major, the Great Wain, the Drinking Gourd:
a way to walk in our ancestors' boots.
We watch the stars as we watch our steps,
looking to take the long way home.

2

When my grandmother read the paper,
there in the back yard, where she watched
the squirrels playing around the eaves
of the barn's tin roof, she sat on a white chair,
until she eased forward to the crackling
sigh of relieved cane bottom.

It's a low chair, made for a shorter generation;
either that or the tapering legs rested
once on rockers that wore out.
Little Roy Burgess wove a new seat,
a simple pattern that's held for decades.
I fended off Uncle Gilbert at the auction

and claimed my inheritance: and sometimes
I ride the chair around the galaxy while I play
my guitar, the jigs and ballads
Great-grandfather fiddled, tonic, dominant,
sub-dominant chords, then back
to the keynote, opening a door to a cornfield at dusk.

And sometimes, walking out on a December night,
I find the Celestial Chair—Orion's rectangle—
his belt, a tin pan spilling,
his sword, corn dropped for the chickens,
Canis Major making a flock of white beaks,
the hens rushing to flashing seed, while Grandma

sits invisible, a dust cloud gathering into a star.

3

Walking down to the bike path, I see
Orion tilting, stretching over
the street from one group of trees to another,
and on the horizon, a white steeple,
shining in front of a trio of skyscrapers—
a Gothic tower, a space ship, a box—

so bright, I can't find the Pleiades
or the Pole Star. The astronomers know
that the constellations are changing,
the patterns bending, the stars light years apart,
so that Orion may become "the Manacle,"
"the Butterfly," or something nameless—

all stories lost: our fictions have lasted
for centuries, the narrative lines forming a map,
there for everyone to accept, revise, or reject,
but now we work at obliterating
the sky—smog, ozone, blather and baloney
our children's final inheritance.

Walking home, I see a row of lights, a constellation
along a hilltop, but so much of what I do
is by dead reckoning, feeling my way
in the dark, until I find a familiar door,
a chair, a book, a place to snudge like a Hobbit,
listening for a tea kettle, snow fall, sleigh bells.

4

What is hardest is walking with a naked
mind into the night, like some earliest
man or woman, leaving behind
the communal fire, the flickering screen,
to go to mountaintop or empty field
and forget ourselves for a little.

When I was a country boy, before I read
about Orion, I saw his limbs and belt
and called it all "The Great Box Kite,"
and I held its string as I stood in the alfalfa stubble,
and a strong breeze kept it aloft
long after I went to bed—and it flies

in me still, when I shine like a clear
sky far from city lights,
when I remember the smell of cows
and a chill wind shimmering,
the tug of the string, the letting go,
the silence where everything is born.

I. Tall Grass

Irving Street

1

A bright morning and the maid clapping for my dance
when she took a break from ironing the steaming shirts,

or butterfly women, my mother and her friends
in long skirts waving their wings above sweating tumblers of tea,
women fanning beyond my reach nodding laughing,

or Granny York wearing a bandana and clutching a purse
rushing out before dawn to take a taxi to the cigarette factory
or Daddy coming home wearing blue and a badge like a flashlight.

2

And one day we moved downstairs,
my mother brought home a sister like a pink grapefruit in a white basket,
and when I still slept in a crib in the dining room,
I heard boogermen in the kitchen making midnight clatter,
the boogers Granny said would come after me
if I played in the street—

Daddy came to my calling offering explanations and saying Hush
pointing to Grandma Spencer, sleeping on the sofa bed
and saying to not wake up the baby.

And another night standing in the back yard I heard
the angels sing, I saw their crystal wings fanning beyond the treetops,
and even though I pointed insisting
Daddy spoke of radios stars open windows,
as if angelic voices coming from upstairs were any less a wonder.

3

And Granny kept white bowls of cigarettes
on her coffee table, and my father sat, clicking his lighter shut making a point,
as they continued an argument started long before I was born

I only heard the words banging together,
only understood a smoking fuming sputtering,
while the boogermen hammered pipes down in the forbidden basement,
coal-black boogers raising a hissing hell as the pipes complained
Bam-dam-dammit-damma-dam-dam-dam!

4

And then one evening
the back door open to birdsong radio music fading blue light,
Mother Father Brother Sister, all of us sitting
in the bright kitchen around the table, my sister in a high chair,
Susan babbled saying something emphatic
then laughed when we laughed,
and we were married then, the four of us
never dreaming of divorce.

It's a spark I've carried far, this memory, lighting candles at another
table where we join hands
John Jane Elizabeth Kathryn Rachel—
the laughter faded away on Irving Street
but it lived, it lives again, beyond the limit of our days.

I Dream of Driving a 1949 Two-Ton Chevy Flatbed

And after Market, we took a road northwest
    from the city, and the heavy truck
    sang high in low gear as we neared hilltops,
    the hills rolling like long waves.

And reaching a crest, we saw Pilot Mountain
    peeking over a ridge, then lowering its round head,
    sinking down among the sycamores
    to watch as we crossed the Donaha Bridge,

And we headed toward the sun, as we passed
    second-growth hardwood and black pine,
    shining houses—brick, clapboard, tarpaper—
    the gasoline pumps, the stores at the crossroads,

The rows of brightleaf tobacco flowering greenish-white,
    the fields of soybeans or corn,
    the pastures where cattle were grazing,
    and pastures given over to cedar and golden sedge.

Just as the sun was going down, a long blast
    on a brassy horn, we glimpsed
    to the right a speck of a house, a bubble
    on the wave rising before the Blue Ridge.

We took a dirt road, we passed dark houses and barns
    and houses where lamps glowed in the windows,
    we rounded a sharp curve to the left,
    coasted downhill and across Fall Creek.

We climbed a steep grade, we rode into the sky
    above the house, the barns, the silos,
    everything below getting dim with distance
    as the Chevrolet roared to the right of the polestar.

Wild Turkeys

Sister and I laughed as we raced over
the grass, the wide pasture,
two fledglings released
from a cage (a one-bedroom flat),
a sidewalk, a forbidden street.
We circled our parents, who were dressed up,
their faces ripe with happiness
as they admired the farm, awash in golden light.

And then I saw a turkey hen and two poults,
heads bobbing, the birds stepping
around a gate post.
I ran to catch them, and the hen flew
screaming over the creek, into the piney woods.

But where did the little ones go?

Wading into memory's tall grass,
I hear their clucking, I hear them calling
close by and then far away.
What would they tell me? What have I forgotten?
I am forever returning, listening
for the sound of laughter.

Whippoorwill

The clear horizon was fading,
and my father and I sat together
on the warm steps,
cinder blocks painted smooth,
Daddy smelling of cows
and a cigarette, glowing, fading,

when it started, a song
both monotonous and magical,
as if God were plying
a hand pump, a musical
machine that said, *Make-it-Flow!*
Make-it-Flow!
Darkness rising from a deep well
and flooding the woods, the corn field.

I pointed, wanting a name:
"It's just a whippoorwill, Johnny.
Just a bird, saying, *Whippoorwill.*"

Still the song rose from the dark,
a siren's voice, sounding
the alarm for me and my father,
ignorant of any danger,
father-son sitting close on the warm steps
and watching the farm fading into the night.

Brains

When I was five,
I loved the curly-headed white-faced steer,
though he was no pet:
he only stared
when I called him to the barbed wire fence.

I didn't see him shot, but I was there
on that bright November morning
when the men attached hooks
to his rear ankles
and hoisted his carcass toward a massive tree limb.
They stripped away
his red and white coat,
the meat steaming, smoking entrails falling
into the waiting wash tub.

I played behind the barn, until my father whistled
and I ran to where
I could see him standing behind the truck.
He told me to get in
as he heaved something onto the bed.
I looked through the rear window,
took just a glimpse of a bloodied face.

Dad took the head to old Mr. Jones,
as sagging and gray
as an unpainted house.
The man grinned a broad, toothless grin
when Dad said,
"I hear tell you *love* brains for breakfast."
"Shore do!" said Mr. Jones,

and they laughed.
But I didn't laugh.
I was sure the man had a row of big jars
on his kitchen shelf, a dark kitchen,
jars full of brains, like in some movie I glimpsed,

jars labeled *Steer*, *Pig*, *Boy*.

Bathroom Music

(Irving Street again)

Granny's bathroom is blue,
except for her white tub.
She says, "Get in and scrub
until you're like brand new."

   Bubble-blub, bubble-blub.

I sit in hot water, poot
so water says "Bubble,
bubble-bub-blubble,"
and the toy boat goes *Toot!*

   Bubble-blub, bubble-blub.

Your Granny's a jaybird,
that's what people say,
so I say, "Hey, Mama Jay"
She says, "Quit playing, turd!"

   Bubble-blub, bubble-blub.

She stands at the door to
listen to me play,
yells just like an old jay,
"What are you trying to do?"

   Kee! Kee! Kee! Bubble-blub.

She pecks at the keyhole,
so I say, "Go away!"
and poot bubbles and play.
She yells, "Turn the key, a-hole!"

   Kee! Kee! Bubble-blub.
   Bubble, kaw! Bubble, kee!
   Bubble-kaw-blubble-bub.

O Christmas Tree

Daddy and I steered the tractor past
tobacco barns
and into the woods, down a road
I had never before noticed,
to a sedge field, to a cedar,
taller than my father.
Cold and cloud cover gave me hope
for snowfall, and the road
curved away among trees hung with mistletoe.

In our living room, Mama, Sister, and I
loaded the prickly branches
with strings of lights, bulbs bigger
than my thumb, and we added
balls, garlands, tinsel, a singing angel.
My job was to check the water
in the stand, red heart, simple ventricle—
I always filled it to the brim.

But all too soon old tannenbaum
dried to shimmering tinder,
and on New Year's Eve, after we unloaded,
unwrapped the limbs,
Mama helped me carry the Christmas tree
to the trash barrel, let me strike paper matches
until the leaves became
a rush of chattering-twirling
sparks, decorating the tree ascending.

The Gift

In the morning, getting ready for school,
she would say, "Look at Mr. Redbird,
such a pretty, vain creature,"
the cardinal pecking at his reflection,
dancing back and forth in the sunlight
on the car's big bumper.

And in the evening, after milking
and dinner and the cleaning up,
Mama sat on a bed
with us and told stories, or she read
Johnny and His Mule, *The Jack Tales*,
a Bible story book.

I wanted to read, too,
but some words gave me trouble,
so she used flash cards:
who. . .where. . .why.
She fed me words until they made
sentence, paragraph, story.

One day, the mailman left
a flat cardboard box, a book about whales,
the blue whale dwarfed
the man who stood beside it,
and fearsome orcas breached into the living
room and roamed over

the gray carpet, where sunlight
was striped by Venetian blinds:
I turned off the TV for an hour and read
my book, while my mother grinned
to herself, as she cleared away her papers,
as she prepared the evening meal.

June

One morning, I walked down
the ditch between young corn and shining gravel,
cool white sand

lovely to my uncalloused feet.
I shuffled toward the giant trees hanging
over the road,

walked right into a shower of music,
as strange as the melodies picked up by radio
telescopes—music from the stars.

I couldn't see any aliens,
but I knew their hymn—*how wide the sky*
was my rough translation,

or maybe the visitors
were merely chirping, laughing at a dirty
blond boy: *a wingless creature,*

how slowly and quietly he moves.
I could tell they were the true rulers of the universe,
making radiant the worm,

the grasshopper, the morning glory—
the singers' babel a blessing,
telling everything to grow.

Substitute

It *was* a long day for my father, milking
to be done by sunrise,
then the noise, the shouting of drivers,
dump trucks kicking up dust,
rushing back and forth between the field
and the wide trench silo—
carved by a bulldozer, the one
that scraped away the apple trees—
trucks loaded by the green harvesting machine
eating its way down the rows of corn
leaving nothing but stumps,
the trucks roaring back to the trench, silage mounded,
the men putting it to bed
under a black plastic tarp, my father using old tires
to hold down the edges—
all the men sweating and covered in dirt,
tassel, bits of corn leaf.

After the fields were sheared clean,
after I brought in the herd, my father went
to do the evening milking.
How were four children to know that the tarp
was sacred, that the claws
of the dog, chasing us again
and again over the black mountain,
would make enough holes to ruin everything?

Daddy came in at dusk,
raged his dead cigar back to life:
with the voice of an angry god,
Dad commanded Smoky to come to the chain,
Smoky the blond shepherd-collie mutt,
Smoky the laughing dog,
and with tail between legs Smoky obeyed,

Dad attached the chain to the collar
and threw the dog into the car, sped over the hay field
down to the trench, jerked
Smoky around and yelled as he beat
the yelping, writhing animal with his fist, with the chain—
and I was the dog writhing and yelping,
it was all my fault.

I sat with my dog long
into the night, there under the clothesline,
until my mother coaxed me into the house.

And Smoky followed the sharecroppers one day,
up to the main road, where he was killed chasing cars.

Sharecroppers

How did the women string the tobacco so fast?
Talking among themselves or shouting at children,
they hardly noticed their hands,
grabbing handfuls from their helpers,
looping twine around the stems,
flipping wet leaves over a stick, back and forth,
the women weaving aprons—
green, gummy skirts for Adam and Eve.

Holding the sticks in the middle to balance,
we children carried the burdens
into the barn, a barn so tall
it took three men, standing astraddle
the tier poles, to fill it from the top down.

Dew dripped onto square tin umbrellas
protecting the burners, the round wicks that bared
their blue fangs in the dark, in the jungle heat.

When the leaf was golden crisp,
we handed sticks, now feather-weighted,
up to the wagon, and then to the top story
of the pack house. Over the weeks,
tobacco floated down through trap doors,
first to the middle floor, and then to the basement,
moist and dungeon-dark, where the leaves
became soft and pliant.

Jake the sharecropper, Rumpelstiltskin in denim,
carried sticks out to the bagging parlor,
a small dusty room heated by a wood stove.
And how did Jake and Betty make "hands" of tobacco?
Wrapping stems in leaf, they seemed to be
making dolls—the handles like headless
dolls, the leaves like golden-brown skirts.

Jake chewed Red Man while Betty dipped snuff,
and while they worked, the windows darkened,
burlap sacks became fat with tobacco.
Two wrinkled people sat under a naked bulb,
man and wife talking of supper
and the sins of their neighbors.

And in my dreams,
when they slapped tobacco hands against
their legs—to check for loose leaves, they said—
they gave me sidelong glances,
for sometimes a few coins fell from the leaf tips
and clinked on the floor.

"Don't tell nobody," Betty whispered
as she raked the money into a purse:
"We grew the t'baccer, so the change belong to us!"

And in my dreams they still come to visit,
though silent now, making slow gestures
toward the fields, tobacco stumps frosty with starlight—
and the couple joins a long procession,
the old people, in brogans, bonnets, gingham skirts,
floppy hats, denim overalls and coats:
no mud on their shoes now to slow them down,
they walk free of every curse,
every cancer, every broken back:
upright they step through the bare trees toward
the constellations hanging like ladders into the sky.

Puzzle

My father quit the farm
one piece at a time:

Kate, the old mule, gone one day,
no word of her destination,

then the cows, thirty-five Holsteins,
sold to a man who didn't know their names,

the tractors, the tall John Deere,
the Ford, John's little buddy,

the wagon rolling on slick tires,
a yellow cultivator splotched by rust,

the antique seed drill,
iron-spoked wheels higher than my head,

a disk harrow, a bull-tongued plow,
the tobacco sleds waiting for summer,

the mowing machine whose teeth
chattered through the alfalfa on the hottest days

and the raking machine that churned
hay into orderly rows,

the manure spreader, orange wagon
splattered black, blades clotted thick,

the two-seated tobacco planter,
its twin trays, belts, and hoses,

the sprinklers, the muddy pump like half
a tractor, the irrigation pipes.

I would come home from school
and the landscape would be changed

in a subtle way
I refused to understand,

the pastures, too quiet, the growing
vacancy in the machinery shed.

One cold Saturday,
my father out for a long haul,

my sister helping my mother pack,
I wandered about the farm,

down to the bridge, along the creek,
the pasture fence, the red boundary flags,

up to the highest hill, where I could look
over the farm and see Mt. Nebo in the distance.

I was looking for a missing piece,
the edges invisible but sharp:

the wind passed through me, as if
I were a wood stove, left there by the road,

the door left open, the wind
lowing over a rusty pipe.

II. Nebo

Then Moses went up from the plains of Moab to Mount Nebo, the headland of Pisgah which faces Jericho, and the Lord showed him all the land. . .The Lord then said to him, "This is the land which I swore to Abraham, Isaac and Jacob that I would give to their descendants. I have let you feast your eyes upon it, but you shall not cross over."

Deuteronomy 34

The Ghost of Nebo

I scrunch and shiver between cold sheets,
until I warm the covers and sit up to look out the window:

On a distant tower a red light flares and fades, flares and fades,
there in the direction of the farm
where I was the prince of barns feedlot pasture pond,
where I was the darling of the big girls who came
to string tobacco or help with the canning,
the cats followed me home
and begged for my sack of bluegills,
the cows trotted to the trough when I called their names.

I was growing almost tall enough to look over the horizon
when it all went empty, everything
uglier than a pond when the dam is breached.

To the right of the tower, a faint smudge, a reflection
from the lights of the city—Daddy's new home.
In a book about the Middle Ages
I found a photo of the tomb of John the Fearless,
on a marble bed a statue reclining, hands pressed together,
so I lie down straight and pray with my hands over my chest.
I pray for Daddy's return,
for a cure for a red face, for a family again.

I pray for sleep—I haunt the hallway at two
three and four-thirty, "To pee a thimbleful,"
Grandma will say, awakened by floorboards
groaning, a flush, a retreat into the cold.

And I fear the Ghost of Nebo, the one who shakes
the windows and breathes
a frosty breath under my closet door,
the old man who was shunned for fighting on the Union side,
who lived in the cabin falling down in the woods.

But when the dial of the alarm clock dissolves
he stands beside my bed,
lifts a finger to lips,
shows me a door in the back of the closet and a ladder
down to a passage, a tunnel, where I creep along,
feeling my way in earthy darkness,
a face like a cloud vanishing behind me,
a red eye blinking ahead—

until I come out to find a low bridge across the river,
a place where the trees emerge from a fuzzy twilight,
where the birds speak to me in Morse code—

so many messages, but they all say the same thing.

The Captain Disguised as a Twelve-Year-Old Boy

No one bothers me
in this old house behind Grandma's.
Just my cousins
coming to smoke Winstons
with me: we flick
ashes and butts into a rusty flower can
(we always hide it under the bench),
say dirty words, eat Clorets before going
in where the grown-ups smoke
and talk about kinfolk.

But it's best just to
sit here on an old quilt with my dog
(he keeps me warm), to sit looking
at old bed frames,
cabinets, planks, to read
Life magazines and comic books.
Vines cover the windows,
shade the wide doorway,
hide me from bugs and cameras
and the ones always
saying *Look at his elephant ears!*
Look at how he stares
at Becky Barns, that girl
who's ignored him ever
since third grade!

And no one
hears or sees the preparations
for landing, no one
knows the controls are
hidden in drawers, that the tin roof
opens up, the shaky
floor boards slide away;
that I'm the Captain of the Martian Patrol.
We're taking over.
We'll do it my way now.

Johnny's Cosmology

Going squirrel hunting, I say: then head out
the back door, over barbed wire then among
horses (the shotgun barrel down), and through

another fence and into the woods, where I
dodge cobwebs, hung between hardwood saplings,
the concentric strands bright with water drops,

thousands of planets orbiting for a while,
until some big lunkus comes crashing through,
then the spider spins another galaxy:

damn! I've walked through the web, through strands
I couldn't see, and the whole thing waves
like a flag: God will probably pull down

our world one day; he'll single me out and say,
I saw you getting all hot and sticky in bed—
you read the story of Lot and his daughters

doing IT, and you thought of your Cousin Jill,
didn't you? Big-tittied Cousin Jill!
And I won't say anything; it's true:

even though I bought a book called *Peace*
of Mind, I never got past the rabbi's
question, *Do men deserve peace of mind?*

Even though I burned incense while my legs
were crossed, I've never been chased by girls
the way the Beatles have: I wish folks could

see through pimples on my chin, through eczema-
crusted fingers, I wish they'd ignore the wingtips
my father bought and would look at the bright

child within, the dimpled boy whose heels
sprouted wings as he chased the cows home,
I wish we could all see our clear souls

shining under brown, peach, olive, black
or ivory skin: but then everyone might see
me thinking of Cousin Jill: sitting

on fire tower steps, I watch two squirrels playing,
the western sky opening, turning pink,
the cars heading home or leaving houses:

I don't shoot the squirrels; no one will eat them,
and we are all rather small, easy to snuff.
So I descend, then wander along a ridge,

find mistletoe, big clumps hanging from oak limbs,
shoot three times and finally bring down my game:
walking downhill, I dodge cobthreads, catch a few

on my face, I stop by the creek and pull
running cedar, then jog home loaded with songs.

Mowing for Grandmothers

1. Grandma Spencer's Yard, Rockford Road

Grandma Spencer shells peas in her kitchen,
while I buzz-cut dandelions, crab
and other grasses out front, where in September
cousins will grab
for the football, stoop for pears,
dodge yellow-jackets. I mow around one side

until the weedy circle disappears,
then the other, but slowly, motor growling
at the septic tank for growing
the grass so high. I mow the wide

back yard up to the first row of the garden,
then step back and forth, the mower
fussing around forsythia, nandinas,
crape myrtles, camellias,
until its buzzy timbre
fades to a sputter, and I trudge in for a shower.
In the kitchen Grandma looks out a window,
turns and says, *Looks mighty fine.*

In the evening, I crawl out a window,
climb, then sit astraddle the apex,
the black-shingled roof sloping, like a golden
eagle's down-sweeping wings, easing over
the yard, the power line,
then over tobacco, soybeans, corn, clover,
pines, oaks, poplars, ferns, galax,
until Grandma calls me and whippoorwills start calling,
while over the grass fireflies are rising and falling.

2. Granny York, Irving Street

A strip by the street
then little squares on both sides
of the stone walk take a few strides
of my broganned feet.

Mower-mower-mowee!
the machine sings under shrubbery,
out-yammering Granny,
who stands arms akimbo watching me.

She walks down her driveway
while I mow the side
yard, long like a dog run but not wide
enough for a Chihuahua.

Granny directs in the back,
motions toward missed patches, warns
of stumps, suspects me of speeding around
the triangular track.

Picking Out

Down at Uncle Bernard's tin-covered barn I stopped
today to watch a man shoe our cousin's appaloosa.
A nut-smashing hoof held between his legs,
Mr. Smith chewed tobacco while he gripped
a draw-knife, shaving the hoof even.

After saying howdy and good-bye,
I walked through pines, ducked under
dead limbs, waded through scrub and briar,
found my way over fields,
found myself at home picking burs
and downy seeds, picking at the fingernails
of dead men, maybe,
Cherokees trappers settlers bandits deputies
bushwhackers members of the Home Guard,
shades tugging at the legs of my blue jeans.

Or maybe these are just the weeds' claws, tearing
at rows of cornstalks and tobacco stumps.

At sunset I shape my fingernails,
leave them long enough on my
right hand to catch strings and roots of the wind.

Tonight my hands are charging
over prairies and blue mountains,
I reach for ballad and fiddle-jig habanera fandango,
I ramble back to Spain on gut strings,
back to England on steel and copper,
I raise my head and call the dusty winds—
over a straight road six strings shining in the moonlight
hands galloping cantering trotting like well-shod horses.

Eleventh Grade: 1971

for Hayes and Gail McNeill

All morning low clouds rain on black-gray hills,
        on flat buildings, where we sit
in fluorescent light, or while we nudge to fit
under walkways' covers.
                        Mini-skirted girls
watch each other flirt with the quarterback,
        while uncrossing legs spark
daydreams, while Mr. Green chats with Miss Clark,
while I sit invisible in the back
of the room, where I imagine rock tunes
        and write, "Richard Nixon
lies/ The eagle skeleton cries": and on

and on the verses flow: while Mr. Jones
discusses the wrestling team's current season,
        while Miss Clark reviews the days
of the week (*loondi, merdi, macradi. . .*),
while equations loom up behind Miss Gleeson.

        But Mr. McNeill walks in as the bell
rings and proclaims *There was a child went forth
every day.* And after class, I show him my song,
        and he says, *This image is strong,
this one flies*: and I sing as I trot to sixth
period gym, though my songs will never sell,
though, instead of baskets, I zap teammates' heads,

        though "my mind has been cornered, a rusting gun,"
though "in freezing rain my soul has bowed like grass,"
        though "my faraway drummer has
                been thumping a practice pad":
I've been alerted, thawed,
        charged, aimed, fired, called
                to march at last.

Nebo

Now leaves dandle light rain,
but among metal X's, the fire tower on Mt. Nebo,
I watched spreading lights
shimmering from Winston-Salem to the Blue Ridge,
while among dusty leaves
cicadas were winding down katydids beginning.

And the country was afflicted by drought,
and somehow I knew
the dryness in my own heart parched the landscape.

It was then the old man walked up from the shadows,
and I felt his steps
vibrating stairs—and there he was,
honeysuckle tangled in his long beard, his robe
decorated with mosses and lichen—
and I gripped the railing as he swung back his staff
smacked me between the eyes, *I'm looking for water, fool!*

and I hid my head among orange cirrus clouds
then stretched under stars and above
the blue constellations the mercury vapor lamps.

The old man grumbled downhill, while I floated, vaguely skeletal:

I float still, but quietly fall to tell you.

III. Always in the Middle of Things

The Death of Superman

On the vast playground, among shouting children,
I saw two boys pulling my small cousin
By the arms, as if launching an airplane.
Playing Superman, I grinned as I closed in:

It's Superman! It's Superman! my heart
Sang as I flew around to face them head-on,
Then *Thump!* Barry's head smacked into my face
And I wailed as I wiped a bloody chin.

A tooth was capped then. When I was thirteen,
There was the abscess and a root canal,
When I was twenty, my left lower jaw buzzed
And stung, until the dentist dug another well.

But the more serious wound still flares tender,
Grows deeper, wider, when I'm not watching.
The paper boy brings salt before I wake:
News of raining acid, driving drunks, falling

Satellites, leaking dumps, a strident mother
Blaming TV for her psychotic son's
Behavior, fathers dousing scalding kicking,
Neighbors turning blank to screams, popping guns.

And Superboy, Supergirl, seem to be dead,
We hardly move in bed, behind closed blinds.
Sunrise brings vertigo, morning sickness—
If we touch at all, we only hold hands.

Meteorites

In the living room an oscillating fan zooms,
                but our faces glisten anyway.
Listen to the fan moaning, moaning,
like a horn
warning boats away from Masonboro jetty.
                That night
of the noctiluca, our nieces scrubbed their feet
on the sand,
faint sparks flying, almost as if
                        running shoes
were grinders polishing the wet beach,
orgiastic
protozoa glowed in the surf, we picked up small
                        sandy clumps,
coals fading in our palms, while meteors
spurted,
the Perseids seeding the atmosphere: seven
                        years later
I rest a hand on your belly, wait
for a knee
or an elbow, or a vibration like heat lightning.
                  Will her life
be a mere flicker, a faster flashing than our own?
She kicks!

Always in the Middle of Things

> "Such harmony is in immortal souls;
> But whilst this muddy vesture of decay
> Doth grossly close it in, we cannot hear it."
> —Shakespeare, *Merchant of Venice*, V, i

Turning, facing the breeze,
the quiet mash of wet dirt buds
manure smoke, we ease into the wind chimes'
ding, dang-ding, the birds' *chee, fee-bee-fee-bay,
wick-wick-wick* flowing from limbs,
the high-circling *keer! keer!*

Among graphite tangles,
above weed piles, grayish brown
then all silvery, we shine at clouds parting
at daffodil rows oo-ing to magnolias,
at starlings greening blueing,
at trash blossoming orange.

Below a sun-pimpled
lake, below a drain's hoarse whisper
wish, wish, we ford last night's rain, this red creek,
talk weeping eyes clear again, until the child
repeats our words, until we turn
from water's soft tug.

And after rocking our
love our child, after forming each
other our scaling clay taking momentary
shape, we float among owls' *whinny*, frogs' *peep*:
Such harmony is in immortal souls
holding fast around the stars.

Cataloochee

Sweaterless, we picnicked by our dusty car,
    watched deer, bobbing like rocking horses over
    the lumpy meadow and into November woods.

We walked a quiet road, saffron dirt,
    followed afternoon shadows to a white chapel
    facing a creek, the mountaineers' only trail.

We shivered among pews, a mildewed upright,
    we touched keys, strings meekly sang of stones,
    rotten logs, winter locking all in mud or snow.

Leaving Cataloochee, we passed a raccoon,
    a ball squeezing under a fence, then a pheasant
    prissing along, then flying, missing her perch,

An overlook, a path to the top of a granite outcropping,
    then a mountain, a wide net free of patch
    or seam, a net seining wind water flesh and bone.

And still the Smokies filter, silent, translucent—
    as we speed down highway or street, as we
    smoke the mountains they leave us bright and clean.

The Squirrel Woman

Once I dreamed of meeting Granny
in an old-growth forest, jungle-dark,
rank with fox and rot of mountain laurel,
where saplings, growing in rows
from rotting trees, stood on exposed roots,
elongated fingers grasping at the loam.

She lived in a tulip poplar as big as a silo,
a living tree but hollowed out,
lined inside with shelves,
all stacked with Mason jars full
of pickles, nails, nuts and bolts,
silver dollars, paint brushes, hard candy.

Up near the crown, I found her sitting
in a parlor by a cold cook stove.
She jumped up and said,
"Where's the kindling, boy?
Where's that firewood you promised?"

But when I emptied my tote sack,
there was a scattering of pencils,
notebooks, ink pens,
paperbacks, pictures of naked women,
post cards, crumpled papers.

Granny shook her head:
"You're a disappointment, always
scribbling, worrying over your play-purties."

And she leaped out a window,
scrambled down the trunk
as her dress changed into gray fur,
as she sprouted a bushy tail.

Sometimes, when I seem to be fully awake,
when I take my jog down to the park
and back, she comes for a visit,
sitting at the end of a limb,
scolding, chattering a blue streak, speaking
a language that can do me
no harm, and then she flits
around the trunk and high into a tree,
far out of range of any rock I can toss.

Lost and Found

for Robert Garrison, 1934-1988

I will find Bob sitting in a director's chair,
        A sketch book in his lap:
He places a wineglass on a convenient boulder,
        Pastels the paper.

All around him streams riffle and breathe, finches
        Settle among the laurels,
Songs percolating through the dark leaves, finch
        Song blooming purple.

I will find Bob in the lower right corner, above
        The title, *Bob Garrison*,
Poete, Poeta, Poietes. On a plate olive
        Green, half a pomegranate.

In his room, the white walls shining, except for small
        Windows, dark squares
Transmitting a city's indigo song, he will
        Spend ten thousand years

Conjuring chemicals into stony calm faces
        Like pale camillias
Or pomegranates halved, offered to the Muses,
        To the starvelings.

He will bid us welcome, build infinite rooms for us,
        Give us pencils and crayons,
All of us makers whose desire never diminished,
        All of us children again.

Shining Wind, Stone, and Tree

At dusk the air turns to blue marble,
and wind sends dark limbs waving,
waving, growing into the obsidian night,
studded here and there
by streetlights, apartment window lamps.
Walking by the high school, I stop to look
at a courtyard, a squared aquamarine,
brightly lit but blurry in wind:
in the center grow two dogwoods, sea anemones
straining the air through their blossoms.

All through the school year I've looked out
my windows, whenever students' heads
bowed to a story and words started to blur:
I've watched these trees, their leaves
slowly burning, crisping; limbs veining
gray walls; then thawing, collecting light.

I've told my students, *Build your minds,
but follow your hearts forever; I mean, look
at this courtyard. The walls are like the things
you learn, the dogwoods are like your dreams.*

I tell them whether they listen or not,
since the wind twirls parking lot trash
and rubs markers and cornerstones.
Since blossoms scatter from tossing limbs.
Since the wind turns on me, leaves me
praying that I'm polished as I'm flaked away.

The Loon

> When full the reservoir is 10-feet deep and contains 18,000,000 gallons of water. This deluge of liquid is kept within bounds by an exterior wall of reinforced concrete. . . .A division wall divides the basin into two sections, so that one section may be drained for repairs without impairing service.
> — *Greensboro Daily News*, August 4, 1929

Before the city covered the Lake Daniel Reservoir,
before they erected a concrete
roof and filled in most of the other half,
leaving a grassy yard and a pond for the geese,
I enjoyed walking the road around the impoundment:
standing outside the chain-link fence,
I could feel the water's weight as the beast
heaved against the walls of the pool,
the water lapping against the sides and the wall
across the middle, the animal
sighing, rippling its skin, as it rubbed against its cage.

One day, when the water was quiet, full of clouds, leafing
hardwoods, dogwood and locust blossom,
I saw a loon swimming—*the Great Northern Diver!*
breaking the surface in places unexpected,
staying under, staying under, like something
I wanted to say, something that refused
to come at my calling,

until, there it was, splashing-flapping-running
over the surface: but it stopped in a *hush*,
stymied by the wall across the middle
and the circle of chain link—topped by rows
of rusty barbs, where sparrows and finches
chirped about their business, gathering
and going as they pleased.

And I saw the loon's peril,
this bird caught in a concrete trap, a reservoir

in a southern city, far from the lakes of the North Woods,
the White Mountains, the Adirondacks,
a pool that looked fine from a distance,
full of cloud and tree shadow—

Maybe the loon—this bird unafraid
of foraging 100 feet below
the surface, enduring enormous pressure,
this migrant flying high and fast, all the way
from Walden Pond to the Gulf Coast
and back again before summer, proclaiming its presence
during mating season with the crooning and laughter
of a maniac, but otherwise given to long bouts of silence,
small wings and feet way back built for propelling,
making the bird a stumblebum on the common shore—

maybe the loon was a failed poet,
the reincarnation of one who disregarded his muse,
a writer too lazy to leave his pond, the wavering reflections,
too timid to go below the surface and, therefore,
condemned to rebirth as a loon,
a squid, a sperm whale, many lives, many
years, before he could pick up a pencil and try again.

I don't know if the loon escaped Lake Daniel Reservoir:
after two days of heavy rain, the bird was gone.
Maybe it died and went down a drain,
the loon sucked into our drinking water,
strained and purified, until a loony essence
rushed from our taps, giving the whole city
a fleeting hunger for crawdads,
grasshoppers, trout, mackerel, perch;
an inexplicable desire to turn off TVs and computers
and pick up *Hamlet, The Waste Land,*

or Dickinson's *Collected Poems*,
(or maybe even *The Spoon River Anthology*,
"Invictus," or "The Weary Blues");
or an urge to snatch legal pads and write sonnets,
prose poems, terza rima, villanelles,
or to sit by the banks of Lake Brandt
and wait for the flights of eagles, cloud bursts,
or a single haiku, chiming at moonrise.

But I'd like to think that the heavy rain
raised the water level, or somebody at the waterworks
turned a wheel and filled the reservoir until the wall
across the middle disappeared: I hope the loon,
taking a careful measure of things, found the right angle,
enough room for a run for the sky, the bird

leaving nothing but a silver wake, the long signature of persistence.

Water Lilies, for Jane

Can I learn to be so
        still, I wondered as I sat all afternoon
in the Orangery: in the first room
        there seemed to be aerial views
of oceanic planets, planets
        dappled by archipelagoes, islands
surrounded by clouds tinged pink or yellow,
        green islands, in the midst
            of each, a small volcanic flame.
The next room, the next world:
        weeping willow trunks swayed
near each end of the long panels, where a lamia
        shined recumbent, her silvery scales
            turning lavender, rose, cobalt blue:
                blue rose lavender:
        as she slept all afternoon
            her face glowing
like a sun fading under the ocean:
        or was it the God of Cephalopods
            signaling with splotches like tree-clouds,
                clouds like splendid gods,
        rotund, pink, amused, dreaming:
            amused dreaming pink
        waterlilies in blossoming lilywater
lilywater seeping toward
                    river ocean clouds
water glowing in homage to blue mid-afternoons,
        momentary calm.
        So here I am now, poling my johnboat
            taking you a little way
through the blue evening: slosh
            slosh: when I was one-and-twenty
I saw myself in Paris, but refused to believe,
        though I sat there all afternoon

soaking up Monet's lilyponds, eyes of blue
    forest green: oceanic dreams:
looking at you, sitting forward, facing me, your back
    to our destination, your face pale in the blue evening:
I can't take you much farther,
    I hear the sluice gate's sighing,
        echo of the estuary's final collisions,
            but we can sit by the gray
water, until water undulates under morning's
    first breath: You can stay if you wish.

IV. Donahaw County

Katy's Sunfish

When everybody is asleep, I float
to the kitchen, grab the oatmeal box,
then fly to my little creek below the plant beds.
I call my fish, "Here, Charlie, here, Pete,
here, Opal, here, Kentucky!"
And I scatter oatmeal the way
Grandma throws feed to her chickens.
In the moonlight the plant bed covers
look like snow, the creek is silver,
while the fish dimple their dimples, which turn into circles
which float into the sky and ring the moon.
Why, I'm not a bit cold, though winds
charge through the budding trees,
it's my magical nightgown that Grandma gave me,
it turns into wool or water or a flying cloud.

Yesterday Daddy told me,
"Youngun, there ain't no fish in that creek;
it's hardly big enough for crawdads
and tadpoles. The tractor wheels
have churned it to mud.
You can't see nothing in that water."

But last night a granny came to my window,
told me what to do to save my creek,
and this morning when nobody was looking
I took the tractor key and threw it
in the water. By this summer, the tobacco
plants will be as tall as trees,
I'll build me a house of tobacco sticks
while chocolate boys chase rabbits
in the alfalfa, and, whenever I want,
I'll float down to the creek
on katydid songs, katydid, katydidn't,

and I'll watch my sunfish nibble at my toes,
I'll tell them to dance a
rainbow moonlight dance, while I sing,
"I'm the Queen of the Katydids,
The Whippoorwills, the Screech Owls,
I'm the Queen of the Katydids,
Katy didn't, Katy did, she did!"

Bobby Jester's Dandelion Blues

When I walked by the quad this morning, I saw
a flock of robins had taken over,
each bird about twenty feet from his buddy,
each running little sprints as they policed
the yard. They were gone when I came back
on the lawn mower, and pushing through the grass
the dandelions were like yellow mice, peeping
from their holes—I lowered the blades and sang
"Born to be Wild" as I cut off their sassy heads.

When I cruised back after lunch, hauling
fuel cans, a push mower, a weed eater,
I found thirty shiny brown hussies
sunbathing behind the girls' dorm—looked so much
alike, I couldn't find my sweetie at first,
but then I saw her, on her hands and knees,
where she was blowing seeds off a tall
dandelion. I drifted over, my blond hair
feeling like it might scatter in the breeze,
just as an ugly, hairy-faced boy leaned
from her window, yelled that the car was packed.

It's funny how you can hardly see the line
on a weed eater when you rev the motor,
but that flimsy thing can chew away
dandelions right down to the ground.
Now that I know what it's like to be mowed, blowed
bagged and dumped, music that buzzes and growls
gives me no satisfaction. I turn off
the Fuzz Face, the Fender amp, put away
the Stratocaster, lock it in its case.

I pick up Daddy's old Martin, pick out
a song about sleepless nights, I listen
to the crickets, to Grandma's rocker creaking
beside me on the porch. In her wobbly voice
Grandma says, "Remember your roots, boy,"
and I nod and sigh, as if I could forget, as taproots
lunge into the dirt, as the full moon flies.

Diana Flora Throwing

I built a log cabin from a kit,
here above Grandpa Mercer's creek, I built
a wood-fired kiln, I dig my clay, I keep
a .38 pistol taped underneath my bed.
While I throw pots in a tin-roofed shed,
Sweetie and Godzilla sleep by the door—
God is the Doberman, Sweetie, the Lab.
       Dad keeps after me to open a shop,
but that wouldn't be as much fun
as going to shows, drinking beer with potters.
Daddy brings orders from his clients, brags
of his contacts, and asks for pieces to match
his school colors, his yellow and purple carpet.
       Cousin Sarah tries to match me with boy
lawyers, doctors, plumbers: she won't understand
and they can't understand why I'm still married
"to a Dago artist who sends no money, only
visits on sunny weekends."
       I mold myself
with a steady hand, and only ask Johnny
Flora for a turn when I'm tired, when the wood thrushes
and screech owls leave me, I listen to a spirit in this
Carolina dirt, on the wheel it tells
slow stories of black pots, hog killings, homemade soap,
milk fever, bloody births, stony trails,
a bullet barking a squirrel from a sycamore limb.
I'm fired by sunlit maple leaf stained glass,
by creek water singing between my thighs,
by a rising tide of honeysuckle bullfrog
cricket noise in May's dusty cobalt dusk.
       Once I found a rusted still, axed, hidden
in the laurels above the creek: I asked Grandpa
what he knew about it, but he shook his head
and grinned—what ghost whispered a secret in my ear?

My secrets have been set free, loud as jay birds
in my mother's Missionary Circle, my father's club.
Glazed by star sand, heavy bottomed, wide eared,
I settle down into deeper secrets,
pull myself up, a silver brimming pot.
So what if I break down, dropped on black stones?
This hand of clay will bring me round again.

Johnny Flora's Dream of Flying

Piloting an antique biplane, I can tell
I've crossed the county line when I see
my reflection in the Donahaw River.
I dive sideways, then skim the water,
find that it's red, not blue, and full of tires
panty hose clocks black spaghetti dead fish.
I pull back the throttle and climb over
tobacco cows corn small factory towns,
I turn upside down and look at how the woods
are shrinking, like green pools down a drain.
I look for my love, find her sitting among
junked cars, dive to fly around her head
but I get trapped in the pot she's turning, a bowl
as wide as the Grand Canyon, I land in the spinning
wet clay and find myself turning in her bed:
I beg her to come to the city with me—I'm making
a good living selling collages, and show
her a silver-tinted print of row houses,
the old neighborhood, a town claimed by the sea,
my mom and dad watching TV in a bird cage.
She says no, of course, and I spin the propeller,
take off from a bumpy dusty gravel road,
a thundercloud, she raises her head to kiss
me good-bye, to blow me over mottled hills,
a strand of the tapestry catches in my machine,
the picture unwinding, both sky and earth: I cut
the engine, try to roll out of the thread, but I
can't stop the destruction, nor the falling of a starless night.

Tommy "Match" Dalton Takes his Break

Man, I feel like I've been rolled up and smoked,
just a nickel bag of local shit,
full of seeds and stems, popping and burning,
hot as a pine knot—I burn hotter every hit.
I'm wrapped in coveralls, glasses, ear plugs,
splattered shoes, tee-shirt, ragged underwear.
I unload fiber, I load thread, I juggle
pirns for the girls, take bets on the numbers.

If I want to sit on bumpy metal steps,
just smoking and watching the red sunrise,
if I sit till there's a waffle pattern on
my ass, that's my business, God damn Frank's eyes!
He come bright-eyed as a Boy Scout, pats my back,
says, "We're a little bit behind, aren't we?
Just pour it on before you take your break."
I says, "Take off your tie and sweat with me, Frankie."

I grinned at him, and he stopped smiling, walked on
to the office to tell his dad, I reckon.
I come on out and lit up a Salem:
Frank's daddy knows why they call me "Match" Dalton.

If Frank opens that door, if I hear a rush,
the everlasting scream of a million
little wheels, a billion yards of nylon,
if he pats me on the back again, I'll kill
that happy-go-lucky son of a bitch!
I'll slit his throat with a utility knife,
I'll torch a box in the storage room
then I'll go to his house and screw his wife.

Fuck it! I want to go home, want to go
to the woods and tend my plants, to the trailer
and try to sleep, though sleeping is hard
when the wife is bitching and babies are bawling.

Though sleeping is worse than working when dreams
are full of chains and belts, Mama yelling
Now see if you can find some matches out here!
See if you can burn the dog house down! and leaving
me crying tied to a tree outside all night.
Or sometimes I dream of rolling cigarettes
as fast as I can, and each one sprouts legs
and runs chased by lit matches—ain't that *some* shit?

Joe Stewart's Reservoir

Bouncing in the back seat of a '56 sedan,
a Pontiac full of Dad's cigar, Mama's
loud talk, I saw it for the first time:
the bright water, the earthen dam covered
by silvery stone. Mama was excited: *I bet
the lake will be full of boats come springtime!*
but Granny sat beside me weeping, looking
below the surface. She whispered, *It feels like
somebody drowned my family.*

                When I was thirteen
on a field trip with the Christian Youth, I went bounding
around the marina with the other boys,
scattered potato chips for the lunkers, the bass
rising to the pontoon walkway—a girl in a bikini
smiled at me, said hello, and I walked away
to hide my hard-on. We were driven down
to the spillway where the preacher explained how the river
used to swell, used to carry off factories, cows,
houses, hogsheads of tobacco.

                After quitting
Appalachian State, I came here and got
a job in this bait shop, eventually bought
the place, this shed sitting beside the docks—
on a hill above my grandfather's farm,
the acres sold and drowned, a river-bottom
place Granddaddy inherited from father, grandfather,
the earliest white settlers.

After work, I walk
to the marina, where I feel the water flexing
its muscles under the floating docks, I drive
a johnboat over to a shallow bay some evenings
and take a dip, stay underwater and listen to speedboats
sing a steady *zing* across the warm lake,
a pop tune, the electrical surge of *now, now!*
and to hell with the past. And on slow autumn afternoons
when the lake has been lowered to flush pollution
down river, I take the boat to the far end
of the impoundment, cut the motor, paddle to where
treetops appear, silted fingers, a kingdom lost.

At night I reread *The Hobbit, The Lord of the Rings*,
the *Odyssey*, over and over, adventure by land
or by water—and one of these days I'll take off,
take a trip to Greece, or to New Zealand—

One of these days I'll walk underwater,
watch the hulls of the speedboats, the skiers'
meteor trails, I'll look for the cattle gap
and find bass and bluegills feeding in the stables
of a rotting barn, I'll feel the weight of something
nameless, while on the surface, the quiet reflection,
nobody leaves a face, no sentence, not a word.

Glory Brown, Her Visitors

1

First it was a loaf of bread or a can
of beans would be missing. Something gone,
something done: a latch fixed, maybe, an armload
of wood stacked by the door.
                              Every time I'd come
home from the store or the old folks' center,
I'd walk in and say, "Hello?" but never once
got an answer, just a whiff of something white.
Me and my black hands shaking, fumbling
with keys and the bottles of heart pills in my coat
pockets—but after a while I got the hang
of it, would leave a meat loaf or a pie,
a scraper, brush and paint, and a note saying
"Door and shutters," then come back to find it done.

Here comes Christmas and I got to thinking
about my helper, some fella out of work,
some poor boy with a house full of chaps,
and I left out twenty dollars and a note,
said, "Take this and buy yourself a wash tub!"
But nobody touched the money—haven't seen
or smelled a sign of my handyman since then.

2

On the day Cal was born, the sorriest of nine
children, I rose from my bed of rest, drifted
like a swarm of butterflies through the door
and up the hill to a clearing: spring was coming
warm, and above a far ridge a bright cloud rose up
and, as I watched, I saw it take the shape
of Christ, King Jesus in a long blue robe,
His eyes flashing, Him smiling down at me,
and, as He walked, the trees bowed to Him
where He passed, He floated by and lay down
in a gully that used to be over yonder,

and He became the round mountain that stands
there now, robed in tall beeches and white oaks,

and the creatures—panther and deer, fox and rabbit,
black snake and robin—all know the sweet
spring that flows from His side: and I look
at how they all come to Him, and I weep,
I moan and tremble, always walking up
and down, looking for my people to come
to my table, before death takes me away.

Millie Greenwood, Deciding How to Pray

I rock the babies, then go upstairs,
leave Julie to her TV.
Julie and Jamie took the master bedroom
when her water started leaking,
four weeks before the second child was born,
and this little unheated room
has been mine since: on a dresser painted white
sits a picture book, opened to flame azaleas,
a silver-plated tray, in fancy letters,
"For Thirty Years of Service at Donahaw Memorial,"
a Bible and a Sunday school text,
pink curlers in a clear plastic bag,
and my wallet, moved from where I left it.

I try to study the Sunday school lesson,
tomorrow's my day to lead,
but the lines just flash by
like furrows in a field when a body's driving all day.

I think of how Julie chased that boy,
then brought him home,
wanting me to be their referee, I guess.
I tell her to believe in herself,
but she doesn't listen.
She got her father's temper,
but he took his independence twenty years ago
to Johnson City, Tennessee.
From my wallet I take his picture,
hidden behind a photograph of my parents,
a place Julie will never look:

A folded photograph of a stern boy, in uniform.
When I first met him, Greenwood's belly was as hard
as a Coke bottle, and we laughed

when he picked me up and danced around
humming "The Tennessee Waltz."
I was his first and only virgin, his honey-lamb,
and he proposed after he saw
Daddy's three hundred acres—have I forgiven this man
for leaving, for leaving
me to sell down to a three-acre plot?

What would I say to Daddy and Mama?
I remember her wearing her bonnet
and carrying baskets of eggs,
I remember him sitting in the corncrib
and singing "Stay on the Sunny Side,"
him shucking, shucking, filling the buckets with gold.

A thudding downstairs—rock and roll on the TV.
Julie turns it down
and I climb into my high wooden bed,
look out a snow-frosted window and watch faraway
red lights, pulsing on the towers on Calvary Mountain
and flashing from an airplane flying west.
Can the people up there see my light?
My white frame house on a hill, above a pasture
where the cedars graze and grow thick?

Should I broadcast, or should I receive?
I've been praying so long for the same things.
I was switched and admonished by upright parents,
I was saved at Shady Grove Baptist Church,
but I am wondering if I'm like an old radio,
a receiver with no antennas, there's so much static.
I know in my heart there's a light,
pulsing, pulsing, beckoning to my false true lover.

Velmer Dobson's Night Out

I saw Albert's red pickup easing down
Old Horse Bottom Road, among sycamores
in the hill's shadow, and I lit out of here
like a turpentined pup, the collie running
up ahead while I followed, my stick thumping
the dirt until we got to the ridge top:
I looked down at the house and saw Albert
walking around with his hands on his hips.

I told Buddy, "Let's go down in the holler
and hunt us some woollyboogers," and he led
us down into the laurels, got me so turned
around I couldn't tell my ass from a bee gum,
my head from a hornets' nest. And it was down
near the creek I kicked against some bones—
I got the fantods, thinking some old man
must've got lost and died there among the rocks.
But, no, it was a jenny or a jackass.

I picked up a jaw bone and carried it along,
like I was Samson ready for any boogers
what might pop out of the poplars or from a cave.
Got tired of stumbling around in the dark, though.
Me and Buddy found a dry place against
a white oak, laid there watching the stars
gathering among the naked limbs, would've
slept pretty good but for Virginia coming
to tell me the cows were calling to be milked.

Woke up to a tornado, I thought so, anyway,
but it was just somebody in a truck speeding
over gravel, the road just a hock and spit
from where we lay, so Buddy and I got up,
relieved ourselves on the tree, and headed
back home, got back here and milked the Jersey
and let her out. Took that jaw bone and jabbed it
in the groin of an apple tree—want to see
if it does anything this spring. Walked in
and found the cupboard and Frigidaire full
of groceries—Albert's a good boy, even
if he does want to haul me to a doctor's office—
then I took a nap in front of the TV,

dreamed my bones were leafing, that I was a tree
full of silver blossoms, blinking in the sky,
as peepers peep and the cows call me home.

V. There's a Landscape That Lives

Chasing Diana Most of the Night,
Driving from Wilmington to Banner Elk, NC

Ripe, libidinous, she rose from a live oak's
low shoulder, heard crowds of nudging pines
making cracks, fled the pecans standing in lines,
the rakes' limbs longing for her easy strokes.

And she didn't stay long among terraced bare fields,
or in bricked suburbs or in beech-oak-sweetgum
woods, or on granite cliffs where ravens kept mum,
or in laurel thickets above boulders' icicles.

I wish that CPA's, lawyers and sheriffs,
farmers, mechanics, cooks and beauticians
had all looked out for the wench, but grayish light
danced in most windows—TV ruled the night—
while Diana melted toward the horizon,
followed by Orion, who wanted one last kiss.

Passing Bear Creek

Riding toward a magenta horizon
        cleansed by a northeast wind,
riding over piedmont swells and among farmhouses
and dark hardwoods, or under limbs
twining and spreading into the sky,
        we become silent,
our faces reflecting the softening light.

We pass a sign, Bear Creek 3,
and I imagine my father opening
a screen door and smiling, then telling us
        Your Mama has supper ready,
a frame house, its windows lit all around,
sits on a hill above a corncrib,
a shed, a large barn. Across a far pasture
Bear Creek flows like a copper chain.

But later, at an intersection, we take the main
        highway, aim to the right
of the Little Dipper, and at a suburban door
my father-in-law grins and says *Come on in*,
while my father sits in his long brick house
half empty—another wife has left—

his house in another city, to the west,
        my mother and sister beyond.
Though my wife's people laugh, though the TV
whitens the room and a fire wavers,
        I find myself
wandering along Bear Creek, below a dark house:
I float through brush, through fog,
among poplars, back to where the stream begins,
just a dribble, a voice barely audible in the windy night.

A Stout One

There sits Dad on his tan sofa,
Daddus Rotundus, watching basketball,
saying hello, but nothing more,
not until he starts talking
of money, how much he makes, how Granny
tricked him out of ten thousand,
how teaching English will take me nowhere
fast. He lights a cigar. He laughs.

I want to jerk this old onion
out of the ground, to strip away
gray flesh and find a red-faced boy,
sobbing because his daddy's strop
stings like hornets, or because his mother
is leaving him with her foster father,
his mama taking the early train
to Georgia to look for steady work.

I want to pick him up,
tell how the Sandman hauls away troubles
in a sack, how Jack caught three devils
and why a dipper hangs on the Pole Star.
I want to put him to bed to dream
like a seed unfurling beneath a new moon.
But he is a stout one, and I have no
words, nor the will for such a cutting.

Barn Swallows

1

While the other birds take off like clunky
bi-planes like Fokkers or Spads
the barn swallow zips away
and around like a jet or faster

like a science fiction fighter craft
guided by the pilot's thoughts
whatever the imagination dictates among
planetary rings moons asteroids

willows pokeweeds flowering hemlocks
over the grass and back
to the mud cups under the bridge
where sunlight's reflections

wave on a concrete ceiling
wing-whir and frantic chirping a blessing
there in the shadows birds circling
perching taking flight

2

They like to feed over quiet water
and I've seen them unzipping
their reflections I've stood atop Fontana Dam
and watched them fly

in from the lake to execute acrobatic loops
down then under a beam
and up to their nests built along
the top of the water gate

on a girder suspended above the overflow
tunnel a yawning mouth
large enough to swallow a house
and black as Hades' gullet

3

And now it's mid-August and they
have deserted their cups
and the hemlocks are dried up
brown sticks of poison

I wish I could follow the barn swallows
to the Yucatan to Argentina
the birds travelling six hundred
miles a day a tide

ebbing as daylight decreases
I wish I could learn their secrets
the zing and zest with which they live
like a thought that flees before I can say it

Egret

1

Against the black pines,
a great egret, so large, so white, wading,
then freezing above its reflection.

2

Every Independence Day
it returned to our pond where it pretended
to be two reeds and a patch of sunlight,
until the splash, the snaky lunge,
the image shattered, rippled, coming back,
the beak pointing skyward,
the momentary swelling of the neck.
How I wanted to sneak in
for a closer look but had no cover,
so the alarmed bird would spring up,
laboring, beating the air,
circling, then heading over the horizon
to another pond, a quieter place.

3

And I imagined the minnows, frogs, salamanders,
all relieved, all gathering in the dark
to tell horror stories
of Snapping Turtle, Mr. Cottonmouth, Big Daddy Bass—
but saving a shuddering whisper for the Lightning Striker,
Death's Angel,
and proclaiming the name sacred, a secret.

4

But here, smelling the shore mud
and listening to the water, the wind as quiet as bird's breath,
I pretend to be the plumed wonder,
and, solitary, I wade in deeper, one step,
then, another—wishing I were never distracted,
never deceived by the radiant image
(a long beak, hidden wings)—
I concentrate, waiting for what's moving below the surface,
a flicking shadow, breathing, moving toward my feet.

Highway 67 and the Old Winston Road

In memory of Jim Wayne Miller

The old timers
followed the high ground to market,
saved their horses, avoided streams, until
the big one, the Yadkin, where they forded, ferried,
careful to keep tobacco dry.
After the Model A,
the State cut a
new highway straight across the map,
from East Bend to Jonesville, thirteen times the
old road intersects with the new, old snake curving
around the caduceus: *but it's
no healing sign:* for at
Lightning Crossroads
or Wiseman's (blinking hilltops), Whites
Blacks, Browns, deacons, heathens, weighty Friends and
flighty kids have all had their close calls, bent fenders,
bang-ups, fiery deaths, while the creek
bottoms catch a few on
slick nights. But as
the Dog Star rises, the ancient
women in hillside houses pay no heed
to big trucks, gearing down or howling past: only
dream of loaded wagons, of their
daddies tacking north and
south, taking all
morning to get to the river,
of boys tipping hats, girls leaning against
burlap stretched over soft and odorous leaf, girls
dangling skinny legs, scratched ankles,
bare feet over ruts in
the dusty road.

Teaching Time

Jack must've climbed a *corn* stalk—for by the time I heard rumor
of school starting, the rows marched up the hill and the leaders
hid their tassel tops in a cloud's belly.   I would've laughed
at gravity and followed Jack, but then Claude Jester came
running from the tobacco barn, just as the wind blew
a wrinkled piece of tin over his head: the thunder
boomed and that was the end of summer: Mom
said, "Soon we'll need to buy you some green
jeans and new shirts, Johnny," and I worried
that my friends would have forgotten my
name, it had been so long since May.
That rainy afternoon, Mama let me
play with a clock she used for
teaching time.   I spun the
blue minute hand around
the red hours, I dreamed
through the years, until
I had a wife and three
daughters. When the
girls were little, we
liked to go to the
science museum,
and there we
dropped pennies
into a slot that
sent the coins
circling in a big
yellow funnel,
we watched
them gain
momentum,
the years
speeding up,
each penny
finishing in
a blur, a
rising *whir*,
and then

clink

A Winter Triptych

1. Fall Creek, 1960

There were snow fountains sprouting
from the grass, snow crosshatching,
erasing the gray landscape,
a boy walking to the milk barn where steam
rose from silage in a concrete trough,
to the feedlot where ghosts floated away
when the heifers stopped their frisking,
the boy running home through sheets
of snow, sleet, freezing rain.

Rain left a glaze he could skate
across in blinding glare:
he dug a heel into the crust and fought
his way to a path his father made.

It snowed three Wednesdays in a row
that month, coldest March of the century.
The milk tanker stayed away from their dirt road,
wouldn't even go roundabout to the easy grade,
so his daddy had to pour
bucketfuls into a ditch between the silos,
a creamy stream, thawing and freezing,:
The icing on the cake! Or so the man said,

damning his deserts, though it wasn't really
spilt milk that made him sell the cows
and take up trucking.
No, it was a West Virginia woman
and the highway song, the steady
hum over shining pavement,
or the machine roaring to the mountaintops.

2. Boone, 1973

When it started, the girls from Florida
ran around without coats
and stopped to catch flakes on their tongues,
but soon everyone bundled up,
pilfered pastel trays from the cafeteria
and slid down a hill on the quad.

Two boys built a seven-foot rabbit
behind a girls' dorm, a standing buck
holding his king-size carrot,
making a promise that would soon melt away.

But the shy country boy believed in Love's
Polar Kingdom, somewhere between
Valhalla and Santa's Workshop,
something purified by a brisk wind,
a world that would not be gone come springtime.
There he might live with Linda, his married friend,
beyond all messiness and subterfuge.

They met at the pizza parlor to talk
about their poems—
after the pepperoni, they watched their hands,
their words, glazing naked limbs
and silvering twigs—
how could such beauty be fatal?

She held his arm as they walked
to the apartment—below a bright window,
at the doorstep, she kissed him on the cheek.

Alone in his room,
he sat in the dark and listened to the rain,
to the trees: he shared their burdens,
felt their groaning, the cracking at the seams,
the aching for April.

3. Westover Terrace, 2006

When his eldest daughter was a little girl,
eleven inches fell in a single night,
the kind that Eskimos might call
Perfect-for-Building-the-Igloo.
He made a rabbit sitting on all fours,
and the girl, wearing a pink snow suit,
got up on the saddle and posed for photographs.

Twenty years later, he called her cell phone,
described the storm on the weather map,
a band of freezing rain, ragged and pink,
swishing toward the coast as if it were a hem
on a dress worn by a flamenco she-devil:
"Get back to the dormitory, and stay there!"

And, for a minute, he imagined his
daughter was a little girl again.
Driving a car, she was hardly
able to see over the steering wheel.

And the years seemed to be
melting, swelling the river of time—
he stepped into the flowing cold
and saw her waving, riding
by in a boat, heading for the rapids.

And he wanted to tell her
that tomorrow's river would find him
poling a johnboat upstream,
the striving against the current

firing his thirst for a spring among the rocks,
for the source, down below Poplar Cove,
water rising as slowly as a minute hand
moving toward the hour—
the moment, dimpled and shimmering,
the day, a dipperful of refreshment.

Wish

One morning as Mama drove us to school
sunrise lit a roadside pasture—more than a silver dusting,
an abundance of glare and glitter, iridescent flash and fire.

But we said nothing about November's first frost,
a treasure scattered over the grass.

Where has this memory been hiding for 50 years?
Why did it lodge like a jewel in vein or pipe,
in a deposit pushed to the surface—by what?

I dream of driving the old Pontiac—
she's a young girl and I am her big brother—
as we reach the crest of that dazzling hill
she takes my hand, she says,
Oh, look Johnny! Can we please stop here, can we stay?

The Calling

1

There's a landscape that lives, that shines
behind a scrim of suburban neighborhood,
behind blue streetlights, the cars coated white:

there's frost on a moonlit pasture, the John Deere,
roadside goldenrod, alfalfa stubble,
a tin roof, a manure pile behind the cow shed.

I rise early to write, as early as my father,
who always stepped out the back door
at five-thirty sharp, his breath a declaration

floating as he walked among the apple trees.
And my Muse, she's a Holstein, she's moaning heavy,
asking for relief, there in the milking parlor,

silage steaming in a concrete trough, a radio
playing the news; a pump chugging; my father
ordering, "Sah!" as he sits on a low stool.

2

And when the cows are walking single-file
to the south pasture, frost melting from
the green path, I'm driving down a highway:

I spend my days tending poems and paragraphs,
while my father would be mending fences.
He always kept his boundaries sharp, the wires

tuned above standard pitch—but I like
to imagine a few loose nails, a stray
stepping carefully over the dangling barbs,

a runaway taking a stroll into the neighbor's
corn, the blond rows, loaded with gold, seeming
to stretch beyond the valley, into another country.

And I'm the one that would not return—
for the land lives in me, the kingdom come,
thawing every morning in the hands of the sun.

A Note From the Author

This book has been nearly forty years in the making. A couple of poems, "Picking Out" and "Nebo," were first written when I was in my early twenties. While most of the poems were written in the last twenty years, many would consider this book a long time coming. I've always been rather slow in some ways: My first-grade teacher, Mrs. Hood, liked to tell the other students that I was the slowest child she had ever seen. For some reason, I would drag my feet when she called me to her desk. But I won't apologize for being slow, hoping that the slower I go, the longer I'll last.

So, thanks to my readers for being patient. Here's my first full-length book, *Cold Spring Rising*.

Thanks to the many teachers and writers who have offered encouragement, advice, and inspiration: Hubie Williams at ASU; Archie Ammons, Elizabeth Phillips, Eva Rodtwitt, and Emily and Ed Wilson at Wake Forest; Robert Watson, Fred Chappell, Tom Kirby-Smith, and Lee Zacharias at UNC-G. And I must thank—along with Fred Chappell—Robert Morgan, Jim Wayne Miller, and Kathryn Stripling Byer, and Appalachian writers everywhere, God bless 'em! A special shout-out goes to Kay Byer, whose support and advice made this book possible. I'm sorry to say that for Archie, Elizabeth, and Jim Wayne, these thanks are rather late, but I must remember their friendship and generosity.

Thanks to my publisher, Kevin Morgan Watson! Press 53 has been a godsend for many writers.

And thanks to long-suffering friends who have read many rough drafts: Sarah Lindsay, Mark Smith-Soto, Beth Rogers, William Oliver, Janet and Allan Speer, and, most especially, Hayes and Gail McNeill. And thanks, finally, to my wife, Jane, and our wonderful daughters; their support has been steadfast.

And thanks to anyone I forgot. Please forgive me. Forty years. . .My memory isn't what it used to be.

I also would like to thank the following organizations whose fellowships aided in the writing of the poems found herein: the North Carolina Writers Network and the Central Piedmont Regional Artists Hub Program, with the support of the North Carolina Arts Council and the program's partnering arts councils.

JOHN THOMAS YORK was born in Winston-Salem in 1953 and grew up in Yadkin County in northwestern North Carolina. He was educated at Appalachian State, Wake Forest, and Duke, and he has an MFA in Creative Writing from the University of North Carolina at Greensboro. He has also been a Mellon Fellow at the University of North Carolina at Chapel Hill, as well as a recipient of fellowships from the Council for Basic Education and the National Endowment for the Humanities. For over thirty years he has taught English in the public schools. In 2003 he was named Teacher of the Year by the North Carolina English Teachers Association. His work has appeared in many regional journals, as well as in anthologies such as *Word and Witness: 100 Years of North Carolina Poetry* and *The Southern Poetry Anthology, Volume III: Contemporary Appalachia*. He has previously published three chapbooks, *Picking Out*, *Johnny's Cosmology*, and, in 2010, *Naming the Constellations*, the last published by Spring Street Editions of Sylva, NC. In 2011, he received the first annual James Applewhite Poetry Prize from the *North Carolina Literary Review*. He and his wife, Jane McKinney York, live in Greensboro, where they have raised their daughters, Elizabeth, Kathryn, and Rachel.

Cover artist **JAN JÍLEK** was born in the Czech Republic in 1989 in Zabreh, a small city in North Moravia. He studied at a technical high school and continues his studies at the University of Economics in Prague with a focus on Business Administration. His dream is to move to the United States and start a successful photography business.

Jan has been involved in photography since 2008 when he bought his first compact camera. About a year later, he moved up to a DSLR (Digital Single-Lens Reflex) camera. Jan says, "My passion for photography has no limits: it is how I work and relax, both at the same time. Thanks to hard work, I was able to become one of Canon's representatives and also one of their photographers. Making photos for one of the largest companies in the industry is a huge success and great honor."

www.ingramcontent.com/pod-product-compliance
Lightning Source LLC
Chambersburg PA
CBHW022107040426
42451CB00007B/162